HAPPY WIFE – HAPPY LIFE

A Survival Guide

by

Robert Lawrence

"To experience great suffering you must first know great love."

Robert Lawrence

This book is dedicated to my loving wife Marianne.

Contact Information

Email: vegetarianpilot@gmail.com

Websites

robertlawrence.org
howtobecomeanairlinepilot.org

Disclaimer: My wife objects to the publication of HAPPY WIFE – HAPPY LIFE. However, because she is devoted to me I can publish this book without fear of significant retaliation. There is a chance that I am mistaken. Just to be safe, if the title of my next book is: "Divorce – A Survival Guide" you should disregard the advice offered in this book.

PROLOGUE

This book is based on my marriage and most of the stories that follow actually happened. My hope is that you recognize yourself or your partner in the pages that follow and laugh out loud because you know what I have written is true. Although I poke fun at marriage in this book, I would marry my wife again, without hesitation. After all, she has amazing health insurance and is responsible for much of the material in this book.

On a serious note, I believe that relationships fail because men and women misunderstand what their partners are trying to communicate. Many couples also mistake early sexual passion for long-term compatibility and commit before they really get to know each other. Can you remember a time in your life when you were "crazy in love" with your soul mate, only to later realize that you were totally incompatible with that person? I suspect the answer is yes. We should be grateful that most relationships fail. After all, if relationships never ended we would be stuck with the first person we kissed in the 8th grade.

What I have learned about marriage is not taught in public school and was not passed down to me by my father. My parents had no advice to share because they never learned how to make their marriage work. In fact, my mom and dad are twice divorced from each other! They divorced, forgot how much they disliked each other, remarried, and then divorced a second time when their memories returned. Consequently, when I was a child I believed it was normal for husbands and wives to despise each other and I swore to myself that I would never marry. I broke that promise at age 32 when I tied the knot with my wife Marianne.

During the past two decades I have learned several strategies to help maintain a happy and loving marriage. I share my personal strategies in this book. I admit that I still have a lot to learn about women and marriage. For example, I do not understand why my wife will be intimate with me, but then forbid me from using her hair brush. She claims that sharing a brush is unhealthy – something to do with follicles she says. I think she is lying. Of course I do not really want to share her brush. I have my own. What bothers me is her refusal to share. After all, we have been married nearly 20 years.

When I was first married a simple disagreement about a hair brush could have ended the relationship. I am a very stubborn person and I like to get my way. As a newlywed I foolishly believed that my wife would have helped me bury a body in the middle of the night, no questions asked. I have since surrendered this fantasy. I now accept that my wife cannot be trusted during police questioning. She is honest to a fault and would rather see me in prison than lie on my behalf. I guess I should appreciate her honesty, but I don't. Fortunately, I have never had to ask her to lie for me. I have my friend Woody for such things. To keep the peace at home I have reached a compromise. I only use my wife's hair brush when she is in the shower, or at work. What she doesn't know will not hurt her. Happy Wife – Happy Life.

TABLE OF CONTENTS

INTRODUCTION

My name is Robert Lawrence. I am an airline pilot, author, sailor, veteran, and a husband. I met my future wife when I was a naïve 30-year-old student at the University of Washington in Seattle. My wife worked at the University. I asked Marianne on a coffee date after we had known each other several months. The coffee date must have gone okay because she soon invited me to dinner at her home. Several weeks later, on a rainy night in Seattle while seated in her 1981 Volkswagen Rabbit, we shared our first kiss. Following that kiss a six-month romance ensued. We even vacationed together in England. During our time together I frequently told Marianne that I was a committed bachelor and if she was looking for marriage she should not waste her time with me. I also cautioned her that I would be moving to California following my long-delayed graduation.

I kept my promise and moved to California in 1997. I drove to Santa Barbara where I knew nobody, had no job, no place to stay, and only $400 to my name. I was carefree and confident that I could create my ideal life.

Marianne was not deterred by my departure and she began flying to Santa Barbara monthly to visit. Apparently, she had not believed me when I said I would never get married. However, in time my thoughts about marriage changed. I awakened to the fact that Marianne is a very special person and I was fortunate to have her in my life. Despite this development, I feared commitment, having lived through the horror of my parents' marriage. What was I to do?

I don't know what really happened. Perhaps Marianne cast a spell on me, as women are known to do. In an instant my life changed. I was waiting with Marianne at the Santa Barbara airport during January 1998. She was returning to Seattle following her monthly trip. As her flight began boarding I suddenly blurted out, "Will you marry me?" Without hesitation Marianne replied, "Yes." She then calmly boarded the plane and returned to Seattle. I was left behind in a state of shock.

In the days that followed I believed I could delay the pending marriage with a lengthy engagement. I was wrong. Marianne had wedding plans drawn up by the time her flight had landed in Seattle. Within hours she had selected a wedding date and finalized a guest list. It was happening too fast. I was not prepared to become a husband. I was scared!

Two decades later I am still married because I somehow discovered how to become a good husband. I learned that a husband must be supportive, reliable, trustworthy, obedient, and handy around the home. I consider myself lucky that my marriage has survived since no "How To" books existed when I married. Instead, like most men my age, much of what I knew about marriage I had learned from television shows like Happy Days and The Newlywed Game, and from watching my own family drama.

What does it take to be a great wife, you may be wondering? Wives must also be supportive, reliable, trustworthy, and supportive. However, men do not care if women are handy around the home. We prefer that women desire us sexually. Men are uncomplicated this way.

I must warn you that I offer lots of generalities in this book. I do so because broad statements are more outrageous and hopefully you will find them comical. Also, by making generalities I excuse myself from having to conduct any actual research. Some readers may be offended by my generalizations. To ease your suffering, when you encounter a statement that does not apply to YOU, just assume you are the exception to the rule.

For the purposes of this book my wife Marianne will represent all wives. She is educated, hard-working, fit, and very smart. However, despite her intelligence, she is unable to set the clock on the microwave, reset a tripped circuit breaker, or even jumpstart a car battery. Nonetheless, Marianne mistakenly believes she is smarter than me because I frequently behave like a teenager. I sometimes have to remind her that I can fly jet airplanes, sail boats, set up our home Internet connection, and do many tasks that perplex her. In fact, Marianne would be unable to open the garage door and drive her car to work if we lost power and I was away on a trip. My wife needs me to keep things running smoothly at home. She needs me to keep her bicycle tires properly inflated and to operate the home thermostat when it dips below 70 degrees in California. My wife does not actually need a husband; she needs a handyman who knows his way around the bedroom. She got me instead.

Because I occasionally enjoy intimate relations with my wife I have to accept her lack of basic household and automotive skills. I have to overlook her fascination with purses, shoes, and clean underwear. I have to accept our differences in order to maintain harmony in the home and ensure she finds me desirable naked. Let's be honest, men get married because we want regular intimacy with the woman we love. Intimacy is the glue which holds a marriage together. Without this sticky glue a marriage is doomed to fail.

I believe in 100% equality for both men and women. Had I been born a woman I would demand every opportunity afforded to men. In free countries I truly believe that women have every opportunity available to men. In fact, I contend that women have more opportunities. Consider this: In the USA, women outnumber men; obtain more college degrees; live longer; and are less likely to be imprisoned than men. Most importantly - women have what men want. Women sometimes get special privileges based on nothing more than their gender. Men get no special privileges. Nightclubs never offer ½ price drinks during "men's night" and nobody I know has ever watched the Mister Universe Pageant.

Men want our daughters and sisters and female friends to succeed. There is no secret male society. If it exists I have not been invited to join. Men build roads, erect buildings, design spacecraft, and create new technologies. Men are great chefs, designers, musicians, actors, and teachers. Women possess all these talents and skills too. However, you rarely see women working construction or highways jobs. Men and women are different this way. We can succeed at the same things but we usually choose different paths in life.

Women remember birthdays and anniversaries and rarely wear the same socks two days in a row. Women shave their armpits and enjoy massages and read People magazine and buy purses to match their shoes. Men don't know if their socks should match their shoes or their pants and rarely shave their armpits, unless they work in a vegan restaurant.

Like I mentioned, women can do anything men can do. However, women don't have to do anything to be desirable to men. Just being female makes women desirable. Men have to work at being desirable. This is why men pursue jobs that hold little interest to women. Men believe the perceived power and higher income associated with certain careers will help them attract women. In fact, I became an airline pilot after my wife mentioned in passing that she was attracted to men in uniform. I am actually afraid of heights. However, I overcame my fear and became an airline pilot at age 49 so my wife could realize her fantasy and enjoy unlimited travel benefits. Good husbands will do almost anything to keep their wives happy.

Men may occupy more influential roles in society but women still dominate men at home. Women control men because they have learned how to tame and train us. The training of men has been passed down for generations. My mother trained my father, my wife trained me, and so it continues. The training is subtle - so subtle that men are unaware we have been domesticated. Women begin training suitable men on the third date. The first two dates are merely auditions. If a man is a good listener and he pays for dinner⁻ he can be trained.

Men are unaware they are being trained because they view the world through rose colored glasses in the presence of women. These glasses prevent us from seeing the red warning flags. For example, my wife appears tender and beautiful in my eyes. However, a spider web is also beautiful, but the web is actually a trap. Femininity is a woman's web. Women construct their webs with perfumes, smiles, or an innocent touch on the arm. Even a quick glance from an unfamiliar woman across a crowded room will cause a strong man to become desperate and weak. Men are powerless in the presence of skilled women. It is not a man's world ⁻ it is a woman's world!

I became entangled in my wife's web in 1996. During my time in her web, I have learned to translate her words when she speaks in riddles. I can read her ever⁻changing mind, evaluate her shifting moods, and sometimes even fulfill her desires. I also know when to stand my ground when we disagree. It is important to stand up for myself on occasion because no woman wants to be tethered to a weak man.

I have learned that women will use emotional warfare to their advantage when it suits them. When I had my first disagreement with my wife I discovered that logic and reason were meaningless to her. She fights dirty and will shamelessly use tears to her advantage. Crying during an argument is like kicking a man in the balls. It should never be allowed. All men know the balls are off limits when engaged in combat. It is an unwritten rule. Gouging of the eyes is allowed, however. A tear in my wife's eye will force me to surrender a winning position because I will do anything to ease her suffering. I will allow her to rearrange the furniture in my man cave. I will yield closet space. I will even agree to watch Downton Abbey with her. Yes, she really knows how to kick me in the balls.

After 20 years of marriage I find myself constantly asking, "Honey, is it too late for me to have coffee?" Or, "Honey, should I buy this shirt?" Or, "Honey, should I take a nap now or later?" Decisions I once made without hesitation now require my wife's opinion and approval. I have become dependent upon her and I don't like it. There once was a time in my life when I could obtain money from the

ATM without having to ask. I once knew what bed sheets to buy, what movies I enjoyed, and how to style my hair. Now I question my every move. How did this happen? I know how it happened. My wife tamed me and then she trained me and I didn't even know it was happening until it was too late.

Chapter 1

DIFFERENCES

Men and women choose different paths in life. Most pilots are men and most nurses and flight attendants are women. Most police officers are men and most school teachers are women. Most hunters are men. Men are more likely to watch adult films. Men are more likely than women to join the military, ride motorcycles, sail boats, and become incarcerated.

Men do not understand why a steak knife cannot be used in place of a screw driver. Men believe it's acceptable to use the same scissors to cut cardboard and human hair. Men believe a frozen pizza can be baked using a cookie sheet.

No man has ever purchased cotton balls or a loofah sponge. Most men do not wear shoes with stiletto heels. Men never wonder if their butts look big. Men never rub lotion on their feet. Men never purchase panty hose and rarely wear bracelets. Men have to be instructed to pluck the hair between their eyebrows - women know this instinctively.

Men wear undershirts beneath their outer shirts. Men buy clothing based on the circumference of their waist and length of their inseam. Women purchase clothing based on a random numbering system that does not account for their height. This makes absolutely no sense. My wife tells me that she can wear an extra-small, small, medium, or size 2, 4, or 6. This must be very confusing to her. When I purchase pants the waist measurement is always 34" and the inseam is always 34". There is no variance. No wonder women spend so much time shopping. When my wife purchases an outfit but waits to try on the pants until she arrives home, and then discovers that the length of her pants is 4" too short, she simply renames the pants "Capris" and wears them without embarrassment. If I reported to work wearing pants 4" too short I would be ridiculed and I might even be fired. Women, on the other hand, can even show up to work without wearing socks. Men never have this luxury, unless they're employed as life guards or waiters at vegan restaurants.

Most women say they style their hair and apply make-up so they will look good for their men. However, men have little interest in women's hair and make-up. Women dress to impress other women. Men only bother to get dressed because we cannot leave the house naked. Women apply sticky goo on their eyelashes. Women are better dancers than men. Women walk their neighborhoods in packs. Men rarely exercise with their male neighbors. Men are often obligated to wear neckties. Women can wear their hair long or short. Men can only wear their hair short, unless they're artistic or employed in a vegan restaurant. Women are more likely than men to soak in a bubble bath. Women can choose to serve in the military, but only men are required to register for the draft. Women can form gender-specific organizations. Women expect men to ask them on dates and also expect men to pay. Women can choose to have a child, or not. Women who stay home to raise their children are praised while men who stay home to raise their children are often considered irresponsible. Finally, the number one difference between men and women is this: women speak an average of 20,000 words daily while men only speak 7,000 words each day (according to Fiona Macrae with the DailyMail.com). That's right. Women speak nearly three times more often than men!

Despite all our differences, both men and women enjoy each other's company and we all want to feel loved, appreciated, and desired.

LESSON

Women: Please understand that men are savages who are trying to navigate their way in the world, the same as you.

Men: Please understand that it must be difficult for women to live with us. I once shared a home with two male roommates and it was no picnic. Also, remember that women resent having to rely on us when it comes to spiders, snakes, power tools, and setting up the home Internet connection. We must be more patient and understanding with the women we love.

Chapter 2

COMMUNICATION

Like most women, my wife speaks in riddles. For example, when I ask my wife if she would like to go out to dinner on Saturday evening she often responds by asking, "Do YOU want to go out for dinner?" Her rhetorical question indicates that she wants me to make all the dinner plans, provided the arrangements meet with her approval. She also expects me to remember the name of a restaurant she mentioned six months earlier. As a husband, I have to remember everything or I will be accused of "not listening." Of course, it would be easier for my wife to tell me where she wants to eat, but this is not how women communicate. Women communicate in riddles.

My success as a husband is dependent upon my ability to solve riddles.

If you are not convinced that women communicate in riddles I offer the following examples. When my wife is cold she will not tell me to bring her a blanket or turn up the heat. Instead, she will ask, "Honey, are you cold?" She does not care if I am cold! She wants me to solve her riddle. When my wife wants me to bring her something to eat she will ask if I am hungry, although she is not concerned with my hunger. Women make statements that are concealed inside questions. This is why men and women misunderstand each other.

It is very important that husbands never comprise with their wives more than 50% of the time. I know with certainty that women prefer strong men, despite their objections to the contrary. When push comes to shove, I will make a decision and stand firm. I sometimes have to tell my wife what we will be doing on Saturday and let her know there will be no further discussion. Then, after further discussion, I tell her I am going sailing or leaving on my motorcycle, or both. I inform my wife that she is welcome to join me. However, since she does not enjoy sailing and fears motorcycles I know she will not come. Before departing I remind her that I tried to compromise but she behaved selfishly and ruined my day. I then enjoy my day, doing what I wanted to do all along. When I return home I often am rewarded with affection. It is true, women like strong men. I sometimes have to lay down the law for my wife's benefit. It pains me to do this. I do it because I love her.

I know that some women reading these words are angry. How dare I make such sexist comments you might be thinking. I make the above statement because all women want strong men. Women are not attracted to weak men! Are you ladies? Of course not. Also, I am 6'2" tall and weigh 205 pounds. My wife weighs 115 lbs. She cannot administer a beat down on me. I behave like a man because I know this is how my wife secretly prefers me. Women do not want to make ALL the decisions in a relationship. Wives don't want to get their way ALL the time. Women want a partnership AND a strong man. My wife knows that her opinion is respected and she knows she is valued. She also knows that in the Lawrence Corporation she is the Vice President, not the President. I have veto power. If my wife wants veto power she is free to find a weak man. However, women are not attracted to weak men, because they secretly prefer strong men. My wife wants me to be strong. She also wants me take-out the garbage and wash her car. What does any of this have to do with communication, you ask? Nothing. I simply went off on a rant and it felt good.

LESSON

Men: You must be strong. Be respectful and care for your woman. Value her opinion and do what she enjoys 50% of the time, but never more. Be prepared to put your foot down, no matter your lady's objections. You must be willing to let your woman leave you. She may leave and find a weak man, but she will eventually realize her mistake. Be strong. There are millions of women who appreciate kind, caring, and strong men. Also, when your lady asks you a question it is wise to pause and consider if the question contains a riddle. If you have any doubts, ask your partner if there is something you can do for her and say that you love her.

Women: Tell your man what you want. We
want to know. We especially want to know
what you want in the bedroom. I know my
wife will seek out another man if I am unable
or unwilling to meet her desires, and rightly
so. Long ago I asked what she desired. I still
ask today and hopefully one day she will tell
me.

Your man is happy to bring you a blanket or
turn up the thermostat or bring you a bowl of
Lucky Charms. Women sometimes feel that
men are distant. Maybe we are at times, but
other times we simply do not understand what
you are trying to communicate. We take you
literally. When you ask if we are hungry we
suspect you are going to surprise us and cook
our favorite meal. So we answer "yes,"
thinking you might bake lasagna for dinner.

Do not take any abuse from your man. If I was
a woman, I would insist on equality! However,
in a 50/50 relationship, there must be a tie-
breaker or you will have lots of stalemates.
Find ways to compromise. You already live
longer, you don't have to fight in wars, and
you get to wear skirts and Capri pants to
work. I would love to report to work without
wearing socks, but I can't. Ladies, you can

only be in charge if you have a weak man. You do not want a weak man. You know it and I know it. Find a good man. Appreciate that he is working and remember that you get to do whatever you want in life and you get your way 50% of the time in a relationship. This is a great deal!

Chapter **3**

RENAMING

I live in a three bedroom home located in Southern California. The home has a master bedroom and two guest bedrooms. Actually, we now have only one guest bedroom in the home. The third bedroom was transformed into a salon several years ago. I say the guest bedroom was transformed but that's not actually true. My wife simply renamed the 3rd bedroom. Prior to becoming a salon, I could enter the 3rd bedroom at my leisure. However, since the renaming I can only enter the salon with permission, provided that I am vacuuming.

Marianne keeps her clothing in the salon. She also warehouses her clothing in the two remaining bedrooms, the entry hall closet, and the laundry room. Her salon is furnished with a laptop computer, wooden desk, assorted jewelry, and other feminine items. None of my personal items are allowed in her salon. My wife simply changed the name of the 3rd bedroom and claimed it as her own. This occurred at the same time Russia invaded Ukraine. I think Putin inspired her. Of course, she never consulted me before seizing the 3rd bedroom. The takeover was a blitzkrieg for which I was unprepared. To keep the peace I have accepted that my wife is homesteading at the end of the hallway. In her defense, I admit to having my own man cave. However, she enters my man cave whenever she pleases. This is clearly a double-standard.

Renaming has other benefits besides acquiring real estate. Wives can enjoy vacations without their husbands tagging along by telling us they have planned a "lady's retreat." A retreat sounds harmless to men and since husbands want to keep their wives happy - we never object to our wives leaving us home alone. While the wives are away husbands imagine it's going to be fun sleeping on their wife's side of the bed, drooling on the pillows, and passing gas without having to blame the family dog.

A wife could spend a weekend away with her lover and her husband would never know. We would not know because we will never call your girlfriends to verify your story. In fact, your husband probably does not know the last name of any of your girlfriends and doesn't know any of their phone numbers. You probably told us where your friends work but we weren't really listening. Because of this, if my wife died unexpectedly tomorrow I would be unable to notify her friends. Worse yet, I would have to contact my sister-in-law via Facebook to share the sad news because I don't know her phone number either. I am in the dark about such things.

By renaming a dinner as a celebration wives can convince their husbands to take them restaurants more often. Who doesn't love a celebration? A simple name change can work to your advantage ladies.

LESSON

Husbands: You must never allow your wife to convert a guest bedroom into a salon. Resist her takeover attempt at all costs or barter for your own private space as a compromise. Any agreements must be in writing as you will eventually forget the terms of the deal and your poor memory will be used against you. Remember, wives are similar to robots because they have perfect recall. That's why you can never win an argument with a robot. Finally, keep in mind that a bedroom is shared space; however, a salon is categorized similar to a women's restroom and you are prohibited from entry in most states.

Wives: You can easily acquire more real estate by simply renaming any room into the house. When renaming a room use vague terminology such as "salon" or "lounge" so your husband is unaware of your true intentions. He will be powerless to stop you unless he reads this book. Therefore, keep this book out of sight or simply replace the book cover with one that says "Instructional Manual" to ensure your husband never reads it.

Chapter 4

DATE NIGHT

My wife and I enjoy "Date Night" every weekend, usually on Saturdays. Date Night obligates husbands to take their wives to dinner and watch a movie. In my home, it is my responsibility to research popular "chick flicks" prior to Date Night. I read online reviews for movies similar to *The Notebook*, *Beaches*, and *The Devil Wears Prada*. Following my research, I present my wife with her options and she makes a selection.

Movies that I find interesting are prohibited during Date Night. I expect to watch a boring British movie set in the 18th century, often featuring a queen. After all, Date Night is for my wife's pleasure, not mine. If I had my way,

Date Night would involve foot massages, delivery pizza, and movies filled with car chases and monsters.

Lesson: Date night is for wives. Healthy marriages must have a weekly Date Night. I don't write the rules, I just live by them.

Chapter 5

WIFE TIME

As a husband, I am required to spend quality time with my wife every week. I personally consider all the time spent in the vicinity of my spouse to be Wife Time. If able, I combine Wife Time with Date Night so I can check off two boxes in one sitting.

During Wife Time I feign listening to my wife while she gossips about her co-workers and relatives. I never offer suggestions. If my wife solicits advice it is only to verify that I am listening. Sometimes I actually do listen. During Wife Time I must occasionally nod and ask, "Really?" when appropriate. I keep my eyes open. Nothing too difficult.

All husbands are required to allocate several hours of Wife Time during the week. It is like jury duty. You can delay jury duty, but eventually there is no escape. As I mentioned earlier, an average woman speaks 20,000 words daily. If women do not expel 20,000 words before bedtime they risk verbal constipation. An exploding wife is never a good thing.

Women can schedule anything they like during Wife Time and husbands cannot object. As the title implies, Wife Time is mandatory, similar to registering with the Selective Service when a male reaches age 18. During Wife Time a woman can force her husband to accompany her when she goes shopping for clothes. This means the husband must drive to the store, of course. Husbands will have to wait outside the dressing room while their wives try on outfits. While waiting, men commiserate with other husbands who are fulfilling their obligatory Wife Time duties. Clothing stores place sofas and chairs outside female dressing rooms since husbands might be forced to wait an hour or more. All the time spent waiting should be counted as Wife Time.

I recently noticed that there are no chairs placed outside men's dressing rooms. This is because women do not have to wait for their men. Wives are free to invade the men's dressing room, evaluate their husband's outfit and tell him what outfit he likes. A husband is never allowed to enter the female dressing room. This is another double-standard, in case you're counting.

Wife Time can also include shared house-cleaning duties. When my wife and I perform household chores together I am responsible for cleaning the home while she carries out important duties in her salon, behind a closed and locked door. She thoughtfully provides me with a helpful "to do" list and checks on my progress every so often. My wife is thoughtful this way.

There is no such thing as Husband Time. I am okay with this because I enjoy time alone. That's why I backpack in the mountains by myself and spend time on my boat. I like peace and quiet. When I am home with my wife there is no quiet time. No offense, but my wife has to get out 20,000 words each day. If she can't reach her sister on the telephone she will have to speak with me.

I personally need to allocate a minimum of 3 hours of Wife Time in order to earn 1 hour of personal time. Each husband is responsible to negotiate his own schedule. When I want to spend a night on my sailboat I must first earn several hours of Wife Time. Fortunately, I am able to accrue Wife Time similar to vacation hours at work. I have lots of Wife Time "in the bank," so I am able to frequently escape on my motorcycle, travel solo to Hawaii, or hang out with my friend Woody.

I remind my wife when I have accrued several hours of Wife Time and I always inflate the number of hours. I can accumulate an hour by sitting on the sofa listening to my wife tell me what the cats did that morning. Later in the day, I casually mention my adjusted account balance to ensure I receive credit. The account only exists in my head but I suspect my wife doesn't actually track the time either, so I am unlikely to get caught when I fudge the numbers upwards.

LESSON

Ladies: Begin the tradition of Wife Time early in your relationship so your husband becomes conditioned to the routine.

Men: Women do not normally require more than three hours of Wife Time weekly. Wives like to see their husbands make an effort. It's similar to attending a Home Economics class in high school. You don't have to submit any homework, you just have to show up and you will receive a passing grade. In time you will learn to listen without actually hearing and become adept at nodding while secretly planning your escape.

Chapter 6

SLEEPING RULES

My wife has full control of the bedroom. In fact, she has control over every room except the garage. She can enter my man cave as she desires. She can rearrange furniture as she pleases. She can even hoard all the cabinet space under the bathroom sink. This is unfair, but I am helpless to stop her.

Before I was married I owned a futon. The futon doubled as a couch and a bed. I accented the futon with a single blanket and one throw pillow. For several years I slept peacefully on the futon with my lone blanket and pillow. Fast forward 20 years: I now have 6 pillows on my bed. However, I am only authorized to rest my head on one pillow.

My current mattress has a bed skirt, mattress pad, fitted bottom sheet, top sheet, a blanket, a sheet covering the blanket, then a protective top blanket in case one of the cats barf on the bed. I always sleep on the left side of the bed, even when we stay in a hotel. I was assigned the left side of the bed because I always have to sit in left side of the car. My wife determined where I would sleep by placing my pillow on the left side of the bed. I didn't make a fuss because I don't care. Only my wife cares. If I tried to sleep on her side of the bed I fear she would flip out.

My wife usually retires to bed early each night. I come to bed whenever I feel sleepy. In the morning I am always awakened by her alarm. I usually drift back to sleep but she wakes me a second time to ensure I have not stopped breathing since her alarm went off 30 minutes earlier. My wife wakes me a third time so I can give her a hug before she leaves for work. This I don't mind.

LESSON

Men: You must set boundaries early in your relationship. If you have died during the night it should become evident by the second night.

Tell your wife to let you sleep unless you have been lying in bed more than 24 hours. If she disregards your request, wake her in the middle of the night and tell her she was having a nightmare and was screaming. Repeat this every time your lady wakes you - unless she wakes you because she is feeling amorous. Actually, tell your woman that the only time she is allowed to wake you is when the house is on fire or she is feeling frisky.

Women: Please allow your man to sleep. Leave a love note on his pillow and slip out quietly when you leave the house.

Chapter **7**

SEX IN GENERAL

Most men are cursed with huge sex drives. Sex for a man is similar to heroin in the hands of a junkie. Nothing a woman says or does is going to change this fact. Men will stay in a relationship with a crazy woman because it has been proven by three friends of mine that crazy women are really great in bed. It is also a fact that all husbands secretly want their wives act like porn stars in the bedroom. This is not locker room talk. Men actually have these discussions. When I run for political office I will deny it, of course.

According to Wikipedia, pornography generated more than $13 billion in revenue in 2014, just in the United States. Ninety-nine percent of that money was spent by men. Men do not watch adult films because they enjoy the acting. We watch because there is something wrong with us. We are primitive savages trapped in the modern world.

If my wife knew how much adult entertainment I actually watch she would be shocked. I don't watch often, but she wrongly believes I am not the kind of person who would ever view adult entertainment. She has much to learn about me. The only way for women to prevent men from watching adult-themed films is to gouge out our eyes. Even then, we will listen to the audio and let our imaginations run wild.

Over the course of my life, I have learned that women enjoy intimacy as much or more than men. As a teenage boy, I was unaware of this fact. I believed that women were above such behavior. I now understand that women want to feel free, uninhibited, safe, and satisfied, just like men. Women who view intercourse as nasty, or something to be ashamed of, are simply repeating misinformation they were taught as children. Prudish beliefs can needlessly ruin otherwise good marriages.

However, an amazing sex life will make an average marriage great.

LESSON

Ladies: Have fun in bed and be wild. Watch an adult film with your man and imitate what the actors are doing. If this statement makes you recoil, ask yourself why. Did someone teach you that sex was shameful and dirty? If so, that person was wrong and their opinion should be dismissed as nonsense. Also, women should initiate sex at least 50% of the time. Remember, intimacy is the glue that holds relationships together. Healthy men will not go without sex any more than a junkie will go without heroin. It is not going to happen.

If you say "no" to your man's advances it should only be because you recently underwent chemotherapy treatment or a close friend just passed away. You can only say "no" a few times before men will stop asking. Men marry women because we want regular sex. There is no other reason for a man to get married. There may be one or two others reasons, like you're wealthy and you laugh at all our jokes. You might disagree with me and say, "Men marry for love." Yes, you're right.

Men LOVE frequent sex. Men sacrifice infrequent sexual encounters for consistent monogamous sex. If you have any sexual hang-ups, lose them. You should be having passionate and incredible sex with your partner at least once, preferably three times weekly.

A quickie in the morning should not be a big surprise. Sex is the easiest and most enjoyable way to keep your partner happy! Men will overlook the fact that women steal our sheets during the night when we feel the loving connection that comes with intimacy. If you are unwilling to satisfy your partner's desires, either leave or give your partner permission to take a lover.

Ladies, if your man is not satisfying you, explain to him exactly what you want. Most men know nothing about sex other than what our teenage buddies told us when we were 16. My dad never told me how to satisfy a woman. I was fumbling around in the dark until I got married. Actually, I was a virgin when I got married. I have to say this in case my wife reads this book. Ladies, you must teach your man what you like if he is an amateur between the sheets. Who else is going to teach him? His mother isn't going to teach him and his dad is still waiting for someone to teach him. It's up to you.

Women, make sure you smell good in all the right places. If you are unsure, perform a smell test. Unless your private areas smell like roses you should not expect any visitors there. Remember, great sex makes for great marriages. Average sex makes for an average marriage. Nobody wants an average marriage.

Dress sexy ladies. Never dress like your mother or grandmother. Men don't want to have sex with your mother, unless she's hot! Look in the mirror. Dress like you imagine Jennifer Anniston dresses when she's home.

If my wife wants me to grow a mustache, I will. I don't want a mustache, but I will make sacrifices to keep her happy. I will go to the gym to stay fit because I know my muscular body turns her on. If my wife dreams of Daniel Craig lying next to her in bed, I will become her James Bond.

Men: Ask your lady what she wants, craves, and desires. Ask her every so often in case something has changed. Always ensure your woman reaches climax before you. Be generous with her and she will be generous with you. Do not be too rough when kissing her on the mouth and elsewhere, unless she directs you otherwise. Make sure you are clean shaven if your beard irritates her skin. Learn about your woman's body. She might be too embarrassed to tell you what she wants, so ask.

You should remain fit and sexy at all costs. Make sure you smell good and your nose and ear hair is trimmed. Also trim your eyebrows. Clean your ears for goodness sake. Shave the hair from your back and neck if you are still evolving or look like a werewolf. Your nails should be nicely trimmed. Your undergarments should be clean and fitted appropriately. You should dress sexy, day and night. Never wear dirty t-shirts or baggy pajamas around the house. This is not sexy. Dress like you imagine Brad Pitt dresses when he is home. Floss your teeth every day. If you're losing your hair just shave your head and embrace your baldness. Make it your mission to please your wife in bed. Know that if you are not pleasing your wife, another man is, or soon might be. If you find that sex with your woman is infrequent, schedule days and times for passion. Also be spontaneous. Be intimate in places where there is a chance you might be caught. Be partners in crime and you will have more fun.

If your partner has told you what they crave and you failed to take action you have only yourself to blame if your relationship goes astray. A person will usually tell you what they want before fulfilling their needs elsewhere. A stray cat will come around as long as you feed it. Once you stop feeding the cat, it will go elsewhere to satisfy its hunger. For those of you who are offended by my words, pull your head out of the sand and accept reality. Human beings are sexual creatures. We were born because our parents had sex. Sex is the most natural thing in the world.

Chapter 8

KINDNESS & MISUNDERSTANDINGS

When I was newly married I once mixed my wife's fine washables and my gym clothes in the laundry machine. I thought Marianne would appreciate my kind gesture. I overloaded the machine and pressed the start button, as usual. When the laundry cycle was complete I hung the clothes to dry. I later folded my wife's clothes and then placed them on her bathroom counter, since I am prohibited from entering her salon. I thought I would receive praise when she returned home and discovered her laundry had been washed, dried, and folded. However, instead of praise I was met with an inquisition. My wife asked what other clothing had been in the machine. I lied and did not mention my gym clothes. She asked about the water temperature, fabric softener, detergent, spin cycle and of course she asked if I had added vinegar. I answered all her questions incorrectly and was gently scolded to never again touch her garments. Good thing I lied about mixing my clothes with hers or it could have been much worse. Sometimes telling a lie is the best course of action, especially if you don't get caught.

Since being married I have learned that whites and colors should be washed separately. I also discovered a knob on the washing machine that changes the temperature of the water. There is a similar knob on the dryer that regulates heat. Who knew? Several years into my marriage I also discovered a "trap" hidden in plain sight on the dryer which collects lint. Apparently, this trap has to be cleaned periodically. None of this information was taught to me in high school or college. I am unsure how my wife acquired this valuable information.

By observation, I discovered that my wife frequently adds Woolite to the laundry machine. I had seen Woolite commercials as a child but had assumed Woolite was used for bathing sheep. I guess not. My wife also frequently adds vinegar to the laundry machine. Before I was married I had never purchased vinegar. Even today I do not know what vinegar actually is or where it comes from, so I never use it.

My wife keeps several furry balls in the dryer. The balls are scented with essential oils, whatever that means. I guess essential oils smell better than non-essential oils. The balls make noise when the dryer is running and they often become trapped in my clothing. My wife never consulted me when she purchased dryer balls. They just appeared one day, like many things around the house. I could have complained about the balls, but I couldn't think of a worthy argument. I must always remember to remove the furry balls trapped in my pants when getting dressed in the morning because I don't want to arrive at work with an extra bulge in my slacks.

LESSON

Men: Never wash your wife's clothing without first asking permission. If your wife grants you permission to launder her clothing, be prepared to write detailed instructions regarding the correct water temperature and spin cycle. Also, remember that mixing male and female clothing is forbidden.

Women: Please remember that men have many blind spots and proper operation of a laundry machine is one of them. By providing detailed instructions and occasional oversight your man can someday learn to wash whites and colors separately. In time, you might even trust us to wash your delicate garments.

Chapter *9*

SHEETS & PILLOWS & DROOL & SNORING

Like I mentioned earlier, prior to becoming married I slept peacefully on a futon. A futon is practical because it doubles as a couch and a bed. I slept on the futon with only my blanket covering me. I don't recall my wife objecting to this arrangement when we were dating.

After my wife and I became engaged I noticed that additional pillows began appearing in my tiny apartment in Santa Barbara. Soon thereafter, she replaced the futon with a bed. My wife had insisted that I purchase a brand new mattress and bed frame at a reputable store. I had argued that it would be cheaper to purchase a lightly used mattress from Goodwill. I was overruled.

Once my wife had decided which mattress I liked best, she informed me that we needed to purchase new bed sheets and pillows. I reminded her that we already had a blanket and a throw pillow, so there was no need to waste money on unnecessary bedding. I was again overruled. It was like being married to Judge Judy.

Although 20 years have passed, I clearly remember looking in the sale bin at Macy's when I was tasked with buying new sheets. My wife chased me away from the discount bin and steered me toward more expensive sheets. She explained that we needed Egyptian cotton with 300 or more threads per square inch. I don't know how she acquired so much information about bedding, but she spoke with authority · so I believed her. As far as I knew at the time, the best sheet was the least expensive sheet. Wrong again. Furthermore, my bride-to-be informed me that we definitely needed two large square pillows. The square pillows had some connection to Europe, as I recall. I was warned to never touch the European pillows, as they were for decoration only. I found this odd as I was not expecting guests to visit my bedroom and comment on my pillows. Of course, I did not verbalize my objections, as my wife obviously possessed vast knowledge on the subject of pillow etiquette and I did not want to appear ignorant.

As time has passed, more pillows have appeared. I recently inventoried my home and counted 27 pillows. Keep in mind that it is just the two of us living in our home, so 27 pillows seems excessive. My sleep pillow is protected with two covers. My wife insists that I sleep with two pillow covers because she accuses me of drooling during the night. When I asked if she also drools, she assured me that ladies never drool. Apparently, only men drool.

Before retiring each night I must remove all the decorative pillows from the bed. In the morning, the decorative pillows must be replaced. Although I am prohibited from resting my head on the decorative pillows, I have to launder all the pillow covers weekly, using only cold water, the delicate cycle, and a special detergent. My wife hides the special detergent so I don't waste it when I wash my gym clothes. However, I know she hides it behind the bottle of Woolite.

During the past two years, I am forced to wear a "snore strap" when I sleep. The strap keeps my mouth closed during the night and eliminates snoring. I would prefer to sleep in the other room, without my strap, but my wife wants to keep an eye on me when she is sleeping. I should mention that my wife also occasionally snores during the night. She denies this of course, offering as evidence that she has never heard herself snore. I have not heard myself snore either.

I often lie awake in bed because I am cold. I am cold because my wife is a sheet stealer. She rolls like an alligator in bed. With each roll she hooks her claws into the sheets and leaves me without the protection of our Egyptian cotton. On the contrary, when I change my sleep position I take care to roll under the sheet, so I do not take more than my fair share. My wife has no such concerns. For this reason, I have labeled her a sheet stealer and a blanket bandit. She proclaims her innocence, despite the fact that each morning I wake to find no sheets or blanket on my side of the bed. Fortunately, our two cats keep me warm during the night. One cat sleeps on my head and the other on my stomach. In 19 years of marriage I have been unsuccessful in preventing this ongoing thievery. To keep the peace I have begun wearing a fleece jacket to bed. Like I said, I would prefer to sleep in the other room and have the bed to myself but my wife insists that we sleep together, so we do. Happy Wife.

LESSON

Men: Marriage means you must accept more pillows on your bed and sofa. Also, you will have to replace the sofa you owned before you got married. Your wife will insist on eliminating any furniture which may have supported prior girlfriends. In fact, your wife will erase all memories of girlfriends past. Don't fight it. Also, you will probably have to purchase a snore strap and accept that your woman is a sheet stealer. Be grateful that a woman is sleeping next to you. You dreamed of a naked woman sleeping naked next to you for several years, and now you have it, so don't complain.

Women: Please learn to change position in bed without hooking your claws, I mean fingernails, into the sheets. This only seems fair.

Chapter *Chapter* **10**

MARRIED SEX

I cannot discuss my sex life in this book because my wife will not allow it. I talk tough but she would poison me and dispose of my body in the dark of the night if I dared to discuss the intimate details of our marriage. However, I am able to write about my friend Mark. Mark often tells me about his sex life, because this is what guy friends do. Men discuss sex and sports and politics.

Mark recently told me that he and his wife enjoyed sex three times weekly when they were first married. I think having sex three times weekly is common in new relationships. Over time, the frequency of intercourse decreases and the sex becomes less adventurous. At some point in a marriage, sex becomes a chore, much like vacuuming.

My friend Mark has to give his wife advance notice when he wants to be intimate because his wife needs time to prepare. In the old days, Mark's wife was ready at the drop of a hat. However, married sex apparently requires preparation. I admit that I need time to prepare as well. That's all I can say on that topic.

Mark told me that before he was married ‐ both he and his wife enjoyed intercourse on his futon, and sometimes on the floor, provided a blanket was used. Now, Mark is restricted to having sex on a bath towel, placed on the left side of the bed, of course. Mark can have sex with his wife in any position he desires, provided it is the missionary position. Also, the bedroom lights must be turned off, the curtains must be closed, and the family pet must be in the room. I think all married couples can relate to Mark's story.

There are two types of sex. There is married sex and there is dating sex. Dating sex is better than married sex. This is why married men watch adult films. We like to remember what sex was like before marriage.

LESSON

Men: You will eventually be relegated to married sex. Married sex requires an appointment, a towel, darkness, and boundaries. You will definitely be prohibited from touching the decorative pillows during married sex.

Women: As long as your man is having regular sex he is happy. He will be happier if he gets to enjoy a variety of positions, some of which may not involve the use of a towel. There is no need to reinvent the wheel. Simply watch an adult film together and imitate scenes in the movie.

Chapter 11

DRIVING

When my wife and I are in the car together it is understood that I must do all the driving. I am a great driver. My wife believes she is a great driver. I disagree. Instead of relying on the side mirrors my wife always turns her head to look outside before changing lanes. When she turns her head she unknowingly steers into the adjacent lane. I have cautioned my wife about this dangerous habit on multiple occasions but her response is to always become angry with me. She can take advice from a stranger, but will never accept advice from her husband. It is probably because she has caught me farting too many times and no longer takes me seriously. I understand.

As a result of my wife's dangerous habits I have to do all the driving when we are in the car together. It is not fair, but I am unable to relax when my wife is behind the wheel. I do not believe all women are bad drivers. I have seen terrible male drivers too. I only mention driving because husbands usually become the primary driver in relationships. It is an unwritten rule. You rarely hear a woman say to a man, "I will pick you up at 7 o'clock." The next time you find yourself on the highway you can look around and notice that men are more likely to be in the driver's seat than the passenger seat. Just saying!

LESSON

Men: You will be responsible for all driving duties during marriage.

Women: Please refrain from giving directions, even if your man is lost. Our ego is tied to our navigation skills. We would rather drive in circles 3 hours than admit we are lost. This personality defect is buried deep in our DNA and we are unlikely to change. Take comfort knowing that with the use of modern GPS devices we are less likely to become lost.

Chapter **12**

CHORES & REPAIRS

Husbands are responsible for repairing everything inside and outside the home. Repairs include silencing squeaky doors, fixing leaky faucets, installing mini-blinds, replacing light bulbs, and ensuring the toilet flushes properly. Wives are known to assign additional chores which are totally unrelated to home repairs, such as spider eradication, yard work, car maintenance, and anything related to televisions, computers, and the Internet connection.

Husbands are solely responsible for the upkeep of the garage. Men should be aware that wives may attempt to invade the garage by placing a weight bench or other items in your parking spot. This intrusion may result in the husband having to park outside. If this happens, the husband will still be expected to keep the garage orderly. Men should never allow their wives to kick them out of the garage. The garage is the last holdout of a once great male empire. Only a weak man will be pushed out of his garage. Remember, women do not respect weak men.

Wives are responsible for decorating the home. However, husbands are still required to move heavy furniture and repeatedly hanging all paintings and pictures.

LESSON

Men: Insist that your wife place her exercise bench in her salon, the basement, or she must purchase a gym membership. Otherwise, she will have control over the entire home. This must not be allowed.

Women: If your husband grants you control of the garage you should leave him because he is a weak man. You don't want to be married to a weak man.

Chapter **13**

CLOCK TIME & DIRECTIONS

I once heard Dr. Deepak Chopra say, "Now never ends." I agree. The past and future only exist in the never ending now. However, modern humans invented "clock" time so we know when the next bus is scheduled to arrive.

Men and women view time differently. My wife sees time as a suggestion, not an obligation. When my wife assures me that she will be "ready in a minute," she does not actually believe she will be ready in 60 seconds. She means she will be ready whenever she is ready. Unlike a bus, there is no fixed departure time for a wife.

If I am behind schedule I can leave my house in jeans and a t-shirt. If I forget to brush my teeth I will chew a stick of gum in the car to freshen my breath. As long as I am wearing pants and have my wallet I am ready to leave home at a moment's notice. My wife, however, has to dry her hair; apply assorted lotions; coordinate her outfit; select a pair of uncomfortable shoes; inventory her purse; replenish her eye drops; find her phone; change her outfit; use the toilet; look in the mirror; apply more hair spray; and then 18 minutes later ask me, "Are you ready?"

Of course I have to drive whenever my wife and I leave the house. If I don't know the directions my wife will offer suggestions, although she doesn't actually know the directions either. From my research I have discovered that 94% of wives are compelled to offer driving and navigation suggestions without their husbands having to ask.

My wife does not have a navigation application loaded on her smart phone. She has no 'app' because she has never learned how to upload apps and she is too embarrassed to ask me to do it for her. Also, I suspect she fears that I will install tracking software on her phone. Her fears are well founded, as I would definitely upload spy software to her phone if I knew her password. Regardless, the fact that my wife has no navigation apps on her phone has never prevented her from offering unsolicited suggestions while I am driving. She once said to me during a road trip, "It feels like we should take the next exit." I was naïve then and I took her suggestion - because I love her. Of course, it was the wrong exit. She then refused to admit she had no idea where we were or where we were going. She is stubborn this way.

I believe that wives offer navigation advice to their husbands because they mistake the front passenger seat in a vehicle for the co-pilot seat in an airplane. Wives actually believe driving is a team effort. It's not. Men would much rather drive off a cliff than admit we are lost. I will not deny this fact. In primitive times men were brave hunters. Now many of us drive mini-vans to the local market to obtain pre-packaged meat that was killed by real men. Modern men have become emasculated. We do not need to be emasculated further by having our women tell us where to go. Sure, our insecurities our illogical, but they are our insecurities and we are not letting them go anytime soon. We will eventually reach our destination, or we won't. It's not the end of the world. Just enjoy the ride and tell us how smart we are and everybody wins. Please allow us this one victory. Or better yet ladies, you can drive. We won't offer navigation advice unless you ask. Promise.

LESSON

Husbands: You should always have something to keep you occupied while waiting for your wife. When you arrive late to your destination you are expected to blame your wife. Other husbands will understand. Install the Waze navigation app on your smart phone so you will always know where you're going and how to get there.

Wives: Your husbands will always be ready before you when leaving the house. Please try to be on time and only offer driving directions when asked. Also, please install a navigation app on your phone so you don't have to guess which freeway exit to take.

Chapter 14

MOODS

Men have two moods. Good moods and bad moods. Wives can experience an endless variety of moods. My wife's moods vary depending upon the following conditions: hunger; fatigue; barometric pressure; humidity level; work schedule; number of dishes in the sink; condition of the cat litter box; smudges on her eyeglasses; number of pillows on the bed; distance from the moon; and the political climate in Serbia. In other words, my wife's moods fluctuate constantly and they are entirely out-of-my control.

Here is a recent example of a mood: My wife and I went out to eat and she arrived to the restaurant overly hungry. As her husband, I was blamed for the waiter's poor service, the temperature in the restaurant, level of noise, and the location of our table. After 19 years of marriage I know that I cannot allow my wife to become too hungry or I will be blamed for all the ills in the world. It is not personal. Husbands are attacked because we are the nearest target. It is my role as a husband to listen and accept blame for all circumstances outside of my control. To prevent hunger related moods it is suggested that men keep healthy snacks accessible in each family vehicle.

Husbands, do not attempt to reason with your wife when she is experiencing a mood. I repeat – do not attempt to reason with her. Never scold your wife when you are driving her to the airport and she tells you that she forgot her wallet. Instead, only offer love and support. If she later blames you for her oversight, accept responsibility and apologize profusely.

Do not expect sex when your wife is "having a mood." Instead, quietly retire to your man cave or garage. If you don't have a dog, get one. A dog provides an excuse to escape the house when your wife is upset with you because her best friend's husband forgot their anniversary and somehow it is your fault, because you also forgot your past two wedding anniversaries.

Husbands should always have several hobbies outside the home. Hobbies provide ready excuses to escape the house at a moment's notice. Getting out of the house is crucial for every husband. It's like having a weekend pass in the military. Sometimes it's good to "get off base" and explore. If possible, take up hobbies that are of no interest to your wife. My wife hates sailing, motorcycles, and backpacking. Therefore, I have a sailboat, motorcycle, and a backpack. I know she will never join me on my adventures, even if I ask.

If your wife enjoys sharing adventures with you, consider yourself lucky. It is great to have a spouse who takes pleasure in similar activities. I support this 100%. However, men must engage in at least one hobby that does not interest their wives. Maybe rugby, throwing darts, bowling, or polishing rocks. Find an interest that your wife does not share and use the activity as an escape hatch, as needed. It's like keeping pain medication in the cupboard after it has expired. It's always there if you need it.

Keep your wife well-fed, well-rested, and try placing 9 pillows on the bed if you notice your wife becoming agitated when the Internet connection slows. Also, keep her car washed, vacuumed, and full of gas at all times. Like any storm, a mood will pass. Hide in the basement or take shelter somewhere safe and you might live to see another day.

LESSON

Men: Never leave dirty dishes in the sink; never throw your clothes on the floor, don't let mildew grow on the shower curtain, and most importantly - purchase an anti-snoring device, even if you sleep in separate bedrooms. Avoid giving your wife any reason to become upset and you can add years to your life.

Women: Please take pity on your men. Keep in mind that men die at a younger age than women. Always remember that men only want to make women happy. If your man accidentally sprays urine on the floor you can teach him to remain seated when he tinkles. Be patient and remember that men are savages. Tell us what you want and we will comply.

Chapter 15

TITLES

My wife assigns titles to get me to do more work around the house. I remember my first official title. My wife promoted me to the position of Information Technology Director. I was so proud of my new title. I was in charge of installing the Internet router, selecting the password, and fixing every problem related to computers. Additional duties soon emerged, all conveniently falling under the umbrella of Technology Director. I became responsible for setting up the Netflix and Amazon accounts on all our televisions and tablets. I was responsible for programming the new digital thermostat; changing light bulbs; cleaning the chandeliers; buying my wife a new phone charger; reprogramming all our clocks during daylight savings time; replacing batteries; cleaning the microwave; repairing anything with a plug; and emptying the vacuum canister. It was several years before I discovered that my Technology title had simply been a ruse by my wife to get me to do more work around the house. I must give her credit because it worked.

Because I am a slow learner, I later accepted a second title when I was appointed as the Fleet Manager. As the Fleet Manager I am responsible for scheduling vehicle maintenance at the local auto dealership. I am also responsible for washing and vacuuming my wife's car, keeping her tires properly inflated, and repeatedly explaining how to adjust the side-mirrors in her SUV. It goes without saying that the Fleet Manager has to do all the driving on road trips, or any time my wife and I are in the car together.

Because I am a hard worker I soon earned the title of Landscape Architect. Of course this new title meant I was responsible for all the yard work. There were no actual architecture duties associated with the title, but like George Costanza, I had always wanted to become an architect so I humbly accepted the unpaid position. With my new title I was responsible for pruning, trimming, sweeping, weeding, watering, and other back breaking duties around the home.

I earned another title when my wife promoted me to Veterinary Technician. Because I am an animal lover and vegetarian it was truly an honor to receive this assignment. As the Veterinarian Technician I have to clean the litter box twice daily, administer monthly flea treatment, feed my cats whenever they meow, and drive to my two fur balls to an actual veterinarian for their regular check-ups.

Although I currently lack other titles, I am still required to do all the grocery shopping; perform most of the housework; do all the heavy lifting; respond for spider removal whenever my wife screams, and of course I do most of the work in bed - if you know what I mean. One day I came up with a great idea. I thought that in order to get my wife to work harder I should assign a new title to her. After all, since titles were good for me they should also be good for her. I broke the exciting news during Date Night. I told my wife that I was bestowing her with the title of Home Escort, which required the use of a towel. She rejected the title. However, she did allow me to sleep in the guest bedroom for two nights. It was not a total loss because I secretly drooled on the European pillows without her knowledge.

My wife has only one official title. She is the Director of Finance. As the Director of Finance she controls all our money. I honestly have no idea how much money I earn, or how much I have saved. My wife assures me that I am able to review our online accounts anytime I choose. However, she can never remember the account passwords when I ask to review our finances. I am satisfied with this arrangement as there is no need for both my wife and I to worry about money. Regardless, with my monthly allowance I have enough money to do anything I desire, provided my desires do not exceed $100.

Update: While submitting this book for publication I have just been awarded a new title. As of this moment I am now the household Procurement Officer. As Procurement Officer I will oversee all Trader Joe's and Home Depot purchases. Of course I have been doing this work for several years but at least now I have something to show for it.

LESSON

Wives: Grant your husband a title to boost his ego and get him to do more work around the house.

Husbands: You are obligated to perform endless chores whether or not you receive a title, so you might as well get the title.

Chapter **16**

SHOPPING

RANDOM PURCHASES:

I have to consult my wife before making any purchase over $50. She tells me this is normal in modern society. I guess I am old-fashioned. My wife, on the other hand, never asks my permission before making any purchase, regardless of the expense.

EYEGLASSES:

Every year I purchase new eyeglass frames. Not because I want to, but because my wife tells me I have to use our annual insurance allotment. I remember a day last year when I realized that my training was finally complete. It was a Monday afternoon and I was at the optical store in Ventura. After choosing my favorite frames I sent my wife a selfie image of me wearing my preferred frames. I then telephoned to ask her opinion. As the phone was ringing I suddenly realized that my training was complete, similar to Kwai Chang Caine in the television series Kung Fu. I had snatched the pebble from my master's hand and there was nothing more for me to learn. I had been conditioned to call my wife and ask her opinion without even thinking about it. My wife had successfully tamed and trained me and it only taken her 19 years. Congratulations darling.

GROCERIES:

If my wife was a contestant on The Price Is Right game show she would be unable to guess the correct price of any food item and would never make it to final showcase showdown. I do all the grocery shopping. Without me I believe she would starve. We keep a chalk board in our home and my wife writes what she wants on the board. I take a photo of the board each day. I visit the grocery store twice weekly and on rare occasions my wife accompanies me. I try to avoid these dual outings as she never compares prices, forgets to bring her shopping bags, and does not even know where the canned pumpkin is located. It's embarrassing.

LESSON

Husbands: If you are the primary grocery shopper you can sometimes withdraw extra cash during checkout to secretly increase your monthly allowance. If you happen to lose the receipt your wife will be none the wiser. Also, remember to buy your wife a special treat every so often to earn bonus points.

If you want to purchase eyeglass frames or other items without first consulting your wife you can lie and say there was no cellular signal available at the store. I do not recommend this strategy as it can only be used once or twice before you are discovered as a fraud. More importantly, wives usually know when their husbands are lying. Save your lies for when you really need them. One day you may need to avoid attending your wife's annual work party. If you are confident in your lying abilities you might tell your wife that you cannot attend her party because you have already agreed to host the semi-annual bowling awards celebration on the same night.

On second thought, just go to your wife's party and count it as Wife Time.

Wives: Always demand to see the grocery receipt to ensure your man is not secretly increasing his allowance by requesting cash back with every purchase.

Chapter 17

FRIENDS

I want my wife to have lots of friends. However, my wife's friends also double as her private spy network. If I accidentally tell my wife that I was working in the yard all day, but I was actually on an unauthorized motorcycle ride with my friend Woody, I run the risk of being exposed as a liar if one of Marianne's friends witness me racing my motorcycle on the Pacific Coast Highway. To mitigate the risk of being caught, I have to be careful that I do not stop for coffee, or visit other locations frequented by female spies. My wife's friends will respect the sisterhood and rat me out, no matter how much they like me.

I suspect that when my wife and her friends get together they discuss new ways to train men. Women are clever this way. Women share recipes as well as taming and training techniques. Women rarely waste valuable time throwing darts or hitting balls. Instead, women use their time wisely, to gain ever more control over men. My wife denies this. However, two years ago I was awarded the title of Massage Therapist immediately after my wife returned from her annual "ladies retreat." Coincidence? I think not.

When my wife's friends come to our house it is best if I am not home. However, if I am unable to escape before their arrival I must assume the role of host and offer the ladies food and drink. My wife likes her friends to see how well she has trained me. At the first opportunity I hide in the remaining guest bedroom and eavesdrop on their conversations. I never want to get on the wrong side of my wife's friends or they may try to poison her against me, or they might actually poison me.

When I hang out with my male friends we usually talk about women. Sometimes we even talk about our wives. Married men like to joke about the number of pillows on our bed, we tell fart jokes, and we point out sexy women sitting nearby. Married men talk with our buddies exactly as we did when we were 17. Yes, even your man talks like a teenager when he's with his guy friends. We exaggerate past encounters and boast of what we would be doing if we had never gotten married. Then we look at our watches and realize we had better get home or we will get in trouble for being out too late. When we get home we tell our wives that we bragged about them.

Men never strategize about training our wives. We are not clever that way. We just beat our chests and tell each other that one day we should get together for a "guys retreat," knowing it will never happen because permission will never be granted.

LESSON

Husbands: When you lie about your whereabouts make sure you avoid coffee shops or other locations where your wife's spy network might be holding a yenta fest. Since you will never be granted permission to attend a guys retreat, tell your wife that several married couples should plan a get-a-way. Your wife will try to only invite her friends, but insist on inviting some of your male friends and their wives. During the get-a-way, the husbands might be able to escape to a bowling alley or sports bar while the women are at the hotel spa. It is better than nothing.

Women: Ensure your husband's friends are married. Married men have been trained and they are less likely to lead your man astray. If one of your married friends is always complaining about her husband, and you are always bragging about yours, be careful. Your friend may go behind your back and go after your husband. There is a shortage of well-trained men in the world and your husband is a valuable commodity. Keep your friends close and your husband closer.

Chapter 18

ANNOYANCES

My wife becomes annoyed when my bath towel is dirty after I shower. She claims I do not shower properly. This is a ridiculous accusation. I admit that I often fail to scrub my feet. I lack flexibility, so after showering I step on my towel to clean the soles of my feet. This irritates my wife to no end, even though she is not responsible for laundering my towel. I have to wash all my laundry. In fact, she is lecturing me about my towel as I speak these words.

My wife often forgets that a savage is hiding behind my blank stare. All men are descended from beasts, just as all dogs are descended from wolves. I never rub lotion on my knees and elbows. I never wear scented fragrances. I never use a hair dryer. I never apply goo to my eyelashes. I have never shaved my legs nor highlighted my hair (both lies). My wife married me knowing that I am a savage, but she thought she could tame the wild beast in me. She cannot. I will continue to soil my bath towel. I must claim the occasional victory, no matter how insignificant.

My wife used to get annoyed with me after I used the toilet. She alleged that my tinkle sometimes missed the bowel and sprayed on the seat and surrounding floor. I could not argue with her. I am a clean freak and I don't like the idea of urine contaminating any area of my house. Therefore, because I am logical, for the past 15 years I always sit on the toilet when I pee. I only sit on the toilet in my home. I don't care if I make a mess at a public toilet because I am a savage.

My wife becomes annoyed when I listen to talk radio while driving. I believe in the unwritten rule that the person driving is allowed to select the radio station. As the driver, I always select talk radio because I tire of hearing the same songs repeated every hour. When my wife complains, which she will, I offer to let her drive so she can listen to "her" station. However, she has never taken me up on my offer. She trained me to be her chauffeur and she does not want to alter this dynamic.

My wife becomes annoyed with me because she believes I purchase too much toilet paper and buy too many socks. I like to stock up on non-perishable items when I find them on sale. I know we will always need toilet paper, so when I find toilet paper on sale I buy a cart load. I do the same with socks and underwear. If I ever ran out of toilet paper my wife would become annoyed. Also, if my wife caught me wearing holy socks or threadbare underwear she would also become annoyed. There is no winning with her when it comes to toilet paper, socks, and underwear.

My wife gets annoyed if I do not "squeegee" the porcelain tile after I have showered. She tells me that mildew will grow if I do not remove excess water from the grout. I don't like to squeegee after showering so she is annoyed daily.

My wife becomes annoyed if I do not empty the dishwasher properly. My wife gets annoyed when I reuse plastic sandwich bags. She gets annoyed when I ask her to stop using the laundry room as a closet. She gets annoyed when our cats bring live lizards into the house. My wife gets annoyed when I move furniture in my man cave without consulting her. My wife got annoyed yesterday when I refused to dig holes in the garden without first seeing her written landscape design plan. My wife gets annoyed when I repeatedly ask where she keeps the envelopes. She gets annoyed when I ask what she is hiding in her salon. She gets annoyed when I ask her to discard the 200 magazines she is hoarding behind her couch. My wife became annoyed when I said her pajamas looked like something her mother might wear. My wife gets annoyed when I am waiting for her outside and I ring the doorbell in an effort to get her to hurry up.

Nothing my wife does annoys me.

LESSON

People are imperfect and we become annoyed by a variety of things. When speaking, it is always best to say something kind, even when you are feeling frustrated and angry.

Chapter 19

HOW WE CHANGE

I look the same as I did when I was married in 1998. Being married has caused my hair to turn grey, but otherwise, I have not aged a day. However, I now listen to Adele instead of Motley Crue. I drive a Honda Accord instead of the Corvette I once owned. I cut my hair at home using electric clippers to save money so my wife can spend a fortune when she goes to the spa. I have AAA insurance in case my car battery dies. I no longer visit Las Vegas or strip clubs. I have pets. I pay for hotels instead of sleeping in my car at highway rest stops. I have a mortgage. I have a primary care physician. I have to watch adult videos in secret. I don't smoke cigarettes or drink alcohol. I have to remember to mail Christmas and birthday cards. Otherwise, I haven't changed at all since getting married.

My wife has changed considerably since we married. She drove a 20-year-old Volkswagen Rabbit when we were dating. Today she drives a new car. My wife owned 5 outfits when we were dating, now her wardrobe fills every closet in our home. My wife lived comfortably in a one-bedroom condo when we were dating. Now she lives in a 2,600 square foot home on a private golf course. My wife and I used to listen to live music when we were dating. We have not heard live music since my sister's wedding 18 years ago. My wife laughed at my jokes when we were dating. My wife gave me back massages when we were dating. My wife acted as if she enjoyed action movies when we were dating. Many things have changed. To her credit, my wife has remained as fit and sexy as the day we were married.

LESSON

Husbands: Your wives will change after saying, "I do." If your wife did not exercise before you married, she is unlikely to exercise after you marry. Unless you remain fit, don't expect your wife to remain fit. If your wife gives birth to your children you will no longer be her priority. Marriage is a team sport. You want your wife to shine. Accept that she is going to age while you remain youthful. Compliment her daily and make her feel loved and appreciated. Embrace your common interests and encourage her solo activities.

Wives: Accept that men will age better than women. It is payback for all the suffering we endured during our formative years. We encountered a lot of rejection before we found you. You can train us, but only to a point. We love you because you love us and because we occasionally get to lie on the special towel with you. Just like you, we like to feel loved and appreciated.

Chapter 20

BENEFITS OF MARRIAGE

Despite the numerous drawbacks of being married (having to always drive, excessive pillows, expensive sheets, married sex, etc.), there are several benefits to matrimony. When I am out in the community I find it useful to blame my wife for a variety of things. For example, if a merchant has me cornered at the Verizon store, I can tell the salesperson that I "have to check with my wife" before making a decision. It is not as if I am lying, because I really do have to check with my wife. She would disagree and tell me that married couples "consult" each other before making decisions. However, it seems as if I am the only person in my marriage doing any consulting. My wife never consults me before making daily purchases from Amazon. She never consults me before she spends money at the beauty parlor. She never consults me before rearranging the furniture and adding pillows to the bed and making plans with her friends. On the other hand, I have to check with her before buying new underwear. Maybe I don't officially have to check with her, but I do. I figure it's better to be safe than sorry.

Before marriage men often go months or years without having a relationship with an actual person. In our desperate efforts to find women interested in us, we have to date. This requires visits to art galleries, museums, and sometimes we have to dance with women at a nightclub. Men will suffer these hardships because we hope it will lead to a kiss, or maybe more. After marriage, we get to sleep next to a woman every night. The sacrifice is worth it.

LESSON

Married men have to consult with their wives before making ANY decision but wives can make decisions and inform their husbands after the fact.

Chapter **21**

CHOOSING A LAST NAME

I believe that married couples should choose the best last name, not necessarily the husband's last name. If neither the husband nor the wife has a decent last name, the couple should choose an original last name. When I married I was going to take my wife's last name as my own. However, I felt society was not ready for such a bold act. Maybe I was a coward then. Anyway, I took my wife's last name as my middle name. Now my wife and I share the same middle name and last name. In hindsight, I should have taken her last name as my own.

LESSON

Don't be a sell-out. Select the best last name, regardless of gender. If the husband's last name is Schnitzel, and the wife's last name is Smith – become the Smiths.

Chapter **22**

CHILDREN

My wife and I do not have children. Sometimes I feel sad about this. However, when I hear a child screaming in the grocery store I remember that I don't have the patience required to be a good parent. I congratulate those of you who put in the time and effort to be great parents.

Chapter 23

SECRETS

Husbands cannot keep secrets from their wives. We tell our wives everything. Wives tell their husbands only what they want us to know. If my friend Woody is having a problem with his lady friend, my wife knows about it, even after I tell Woody that his secret is safe with me. Since Woody was once married he should know that his secrets are safe with me - and my wife. Of course, this means that Woody's secrets are not safe, as my wife cannot keep a secret either.

If my brother was a wanted fugitive and I was the only person alive who knew of his whereabouts, within minutes my wife would also know his whereabouts. If there was a reward she might turn him in.

I cannot keep any secrets from my wife because sex is a natural truth serum. I am an open book as long as my wife and I are having regular meetings on the towel. This is why the Russian government uses sexy female spies to obtain State secrets from high ranking American men.

Unlike men, wives keep all kinds of secrets from their husbands. I don't even know what my wife purchases online because I am not allowed to open the packages that arrive daily from Zappos. My wife assures me that she is only ordering toothpaste and dental floss. We must be using lots of toothpaste given the number of packages arriving at our home. I suspect my wife is secretly ordering clothing. However, I cannot confirm this because the packages are immediately taken to her salon where they are opened out-of-sight. She is sneaky this way.

Chapter 24

TROUBLE

WHAT GETS HUSBANDS IN TROUBLE:

As a husband I can get in trouble for washing dishes incorrectly; washing my wives clothing; not enough foreplay; too much foreplay; watching too much television; not spending enough time at home; spending too much time at home; failure to mind read; mind reading; being a man; fart jokes; actual farting; talking with other women; looking at women – even on television; forgetting birthdays; forgetting anniversaries; wrong gift; not consulting wife on gift; not surprising wife with gift; emptying dish washer and not returning dishes to correct location; driving too fast; not asking directions; not shaving; not looking like Brad

Pitt; being out of shape; getting in shape; not being friendly; being too friendly; asking for sex; not asking for sex; not asking about her day; not listening; offering advice when I should only listen; thinking that a hug means she wants sex; feeling her up when she just wants to be held; not knowing how to dab out a stain; not knowing all the uses of vinegar; eating off the good plates; not noticing her new outfit; asking the cost of the outfit; not noticing a new hair style; and not wearing the scarf she bought me.

WHAT GETS WIVES IN TROUBLE:

Nothing!

LESSON

Husbands: Women can do nothing wrong and men do most things wrong.

Wives: If your man gets in trouble it's your fault. You are responsible for taming and training your man. If a football team loses every game it is the coach who is fired. The buck stops with you ladies. When your husband is constantly misbehaving you should consult with your coven and find new ways to train your savage. If I can be trained, any man can be trained.

CONCLUSION

I have pulled back the curtain and shared secrets that will allow wives to better understand their husbands and help husbands satisfy their wives. Wives have been reminded that men are sex-obsessed savages who dearly want to keep them happy. Men have learned that women speak in riddles, they tame and train us, and use tears to get their way. By understanding our partners we can improve our relationships. We are lucky to have each other.

Husbands: You should always ask your wife about her day. Also, program your phone to vibrate hourly when you are home so you are reminded to acknowledge your wife. When my phone vibrates I usually yell across the room and say, "I love you honey" or "Thanks for being a great wife." She enjoys hearing me say that I love her. I score points and it costs me nothing.

Tell your wife what you appreciate about her. Make your woman feel safe, loved, and valued. Do whatever it takes to maintain intimacy. Schedule time on the towel if that's what it takes. It is hard to be angry when you are both naked. Always satisfy your wife before you satisfy yourself. Ask your wife what she wants. Accumulate Wife Time early in the week so you can escape on weekends. Plan a weekly Date Night and watch movies that your wife enjoys. Be nice to her friends and family. When in doubt, be kind. Understand that women speak in riddles and remember to pause and attempt to translate her words before speaking. Keep yourself sexy and dress like you are still trying to win her over. Insist on titles for all the work you're obligated to do around the house. Never surrender the garage and don't allow your wife to rename rooms in the house. Write down all the uses of vinegar and the location of envelopes so you don't have to ask repeatedly. Accept that women like pillows and high thread count sheets. Sit down when you pee at home. Do all the shopping so you can get cash back at the register and increase your allowance. Have lots of hobbies that your wife doesn't share so you can get out of the house more often. Get a dog so you can escape at a moment's notice. Treat your wife as a full partner, but never let her get her way more than 50% of the time or she will lose her respect for you. Exaggerate how much Wife Time you have accumulated.

Women: Give your men titles. Rename rooms to make them your own. Try to mix your money so you can control the finances. Stay fit. Keep things spicy and spend more time on the towel and elsewhere. Tell your man what you want. Remember that your man wants to make you happy. Avoid speaking in riddles if you can. Never offer navigation advice while driving unless you have a map or driving application on your phone. Never wear an outfit your grandmother or mother might wear. Plan a lady's retreat to get time apart from your husband. Teach your man how to properly operate the laundry machine and instruct him how to dab out a stain using only water and vinegar.

ABOUT THE AUTHOR

ROBERT LAWRENCE is an airline pilot, sailor, adventurer, and an author of several books. He served in the US Army 3/75th Airborne Ranger Regiment from 1985-86 and is a graduate of the University of Washington in Seattle. He currently lives in Southern California with his wife and two rescue cats.

Other books by Robert Lawrence

- A BETTER LIFE: Goal Setting, Visualization, & The Law Of Attraction
- HOW TO BECOME AN AIRLINE PILOT: Achieve Your Dream Without Going Broke
- A Day In The Life Of An Airline Pilot

Please take a moment and leave a positive 5-star review wherever you purchased this book. It will mean a lot to me. I am grateful for your support.

https://www.amazon.com/review/create-review/ref=cm_cr_dp_d_wr_but_top?ie=UTF8&channel=glance-detail&asin=0999383914#

Some of My Favorite Authors & Speakers

Dr. Wayne Dyer
Jack Canfield
Esther Hicks
Louise Hay
Napoleon Hill
Drew Bycoskie
Marc Allen
Les Brown
Deepak Chopra
Bob Proctor
Earl Nightingale
Richard Bach
Joe Vitale
Claude Bristol
Neville Goddard

Podcasts I Enjoy

Join Up Dots with David Ralph
The Hidden Why with Leigh Martinuzzi
The Joe Rogan Experience
Inspire Nation with Michael Sandler
The Sean Croxton Sessions
Unleash Your Passion & Step Into Greatness with Drew
Bycoskie
The James Altucher Show
MichelleNgome.com
Theater Of The Mind With Kelly Howell
Big Whig Nation with Darrin Bentley
Adam Carolla Show
Duncan Trussell Family Hour

Favorite Songs On My iPod

Hazy Days by Gabe Lopez
There's Nothing Holdin' Me Back by Sean Mendes

Favorite YouTube Channels

YouAreCreators
Your Youniverse

Recommendations

I highly recommend Sheppard Air for your pilot testing and study needs.
Visit their website at Sheppardair.com

I highly recommend Greg Guz for all your digital marketing solutions.
Visit his website at www.gmguz.com

Printed in Great Britain
by Amazon

32982403R00067